EMMITT
RUN WITH HISTORY™

Primary Photography by Ron St. Angelo

Edited by Reagan White

Produced and Published by The Calvert Group

Emmitt Run With History Trademark ™ 2002 by EmmittZone, Inc.
Copyright © 2002 by The Calvert Group. All rights reserved.
This product is officially licensed by EmmittZone, Inc. EmmittZone logo and E22 football are registered trademarks of AMG & EmmittZone, Inc.

Library of Congress Cataloging-in-Publication Data:
Smith, Emmitt
Published by: The Calvert Group
200 Crescent Court, Suite 620, Dallas, Texas 75201
ISBN: 0-9725042-0-6
First Edition: November 2002
www.thecalvertgroup.com

"This book is dedicated to all those that contributed to my lifelong Run With History. God has truly blessed us all."
— Emmitt Smith

My husband,

Baby, I often remind others of my love for you and what a blessing you are to our children and me. However, this is my moment to express in written form, my sincere appreciation for the love you have for me. It's so apparent, not by the things you do, but the love in your eyes each time we are together.

I am so proud of what God is doing in your life, you were chosen to walk in greatness, and this is your moment.

Thanks for sharing you with me.

Love,
Your wife

I don't think that anyone could have taken more pride in talking about Emmitt than my husband, Walter Payton.

Walter gravitated towards fellow athletes that displayed the same passion, drive and love for football that he possessed. Who they were off the football field was even more important. In Walter's eyes, Emmitt was all of the above, and then some.

Emmitt Smith breaking Walter's rushing record was inevitable. Our son Jarrett and daughter Brittney said, "Go for it!" Walter's motto was that records are made to be broken and that drove him to greater heights.

Emmitt's many accomplishments in a Dallas Cowboys uniform speak volumes. Truly great athletes think alike. Ironically, Walter had even mentioned that if anyone was going to break his rushing record he felt it would be Emmitt Smith. How's that for insight?

Off the football field, Emmitt continues to mirror the likeness of Walter by extending a helping hand to those who we've entrusted with the future — our children. Making a difference in the lives of children was a mission Walter did not take lightly, and it was certainly one he received the most self-satisfaction from. Through Emmitt's involvement with "The Open Doors Foundation", "Make A Wish Foundation" and other similar charitable organizations, Emmitt emulates Walter's hands-on giving to children.

This summer my family and I were fortunate to spend time with Emmitt and his family. In conversation he reminisced about discussing football with Walter and how he looked to him as his mentor. At that time he told my son, Jarrett, to call him any time if he felt the need for a mentor. Again, I see Walter. Emmitt didn't wait for a call. Instead he recently called Jarrett at school with kind words and stressed the importance of keeping a positive attitude. Emmitt, your words and actions continually prove to be genuine and sincere, and for this I personally thank you.

Walter is revered in the sports world as one of NFL's greatest players. But what was truly important to him was his interaction with everyday people. He never stopped being just an ordinary man who personally touched so many lives. "Sweetness" said it all. The traits everyone grew to love about him are very much alive in you. Emmitt, you too, are making your mark and creating your own legacy and I am truly proud and honored to be your friend.

God has blessed you and Pat with a wonderful family, and I pray he continues to bless you with good health, surround you with true friends, and for all the goodness in your heart.

Connie Payton

EMMITT
RUN WITH HISTORY™

The Record — 8
What the record means to him and the great
running backs he's passed along the way

The Legends — 20
The men he's supplanted

The Defining Moments — 34
Four games that defined his career

The Early Years — 48
Escambia and Florida years

The Chase — 66
Season by season with the Cowboys

The Man — 110
Family life and behind the scenes

The Numbers — 126
Escambia, Florida and Cowboys numbers overview

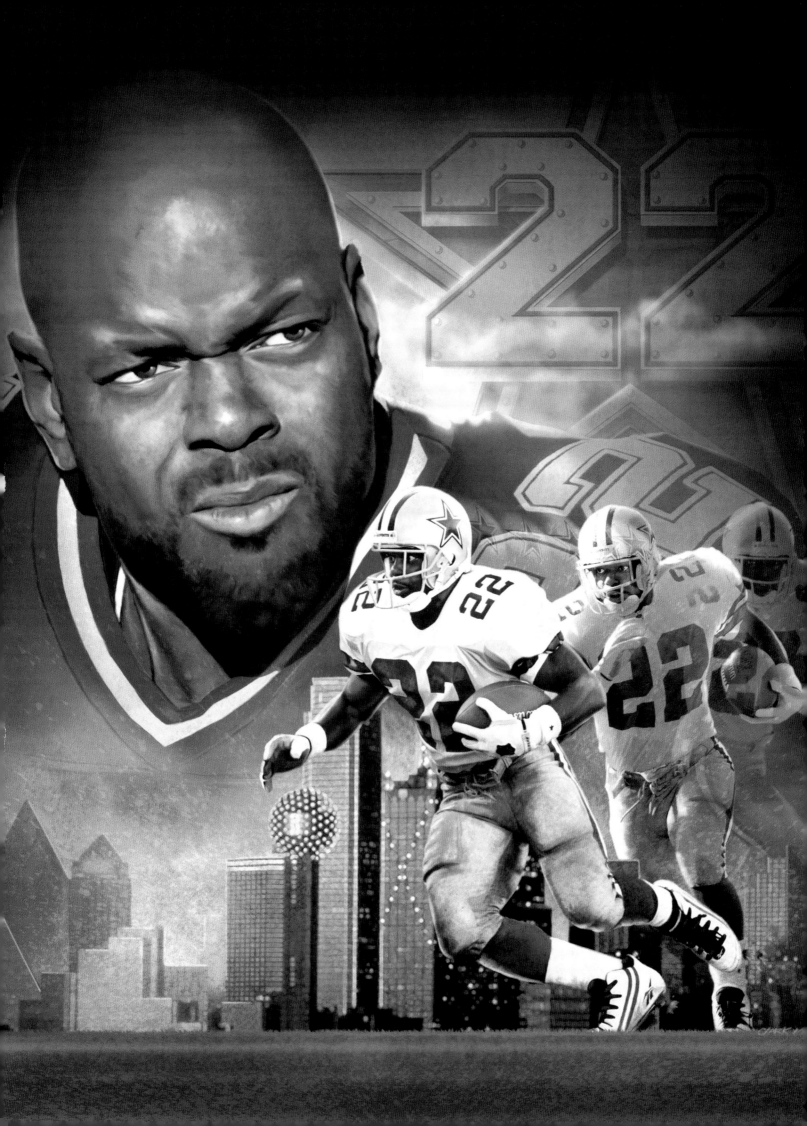

THE RECORD
16,743 (and counting)

"It was very important to me to break

the record at Texas Stadium

because this is where it all began."

— Emmitt Smith

*"I wanted to jump around and celebrate
a lot more, but we had a game to win
and I needed to compose myself
long enough to get focused on the Seahawks."
— Emmitt Smith*

Michael Irvin was the first to actually see it written down. "Become the NFL's all-time rushing leader." Of course, the act would be more difficult than any of us will ever realize.

Irvin read those words in 1990 before Emmitt, fresh off the campus of the University of Florida, had ever taken a handoff in the NFL.

"Yeah, I thought he was kidding," remembers Irvin, the Cowboys former Pro Bowl wide receiver. "But when I said something to him about it, he looked as serious as he does on game day. He really believes in himself and he's made it happen."

Thirteen seasons of determination followed that simple sentence; and now, Emmitt Smith is the NFL's all-time rushing leader, supplanting his idol, Walter Payton. Emmitt is at the top of a list that includes such luminaries as Jim Brown, Gale Sayers, Barry Sanders, Earl Campbell, Marcus Allen, John Riggins, and Eric Dickerson. Amazingly, Emmitt Smith looks up at none of them.

The record-breaking run against the Seattle Seahawks on October 27, 2002, in Texas Stadium was truly a special moment and will never be forgotten. It will be played and replayed on NFL Films indefinitely.

The title came on a play designated as 15 Lead, which resulted in an 11-yard gain on 2nd and 7 from the Cowboys 30-yard line with 9:10 left in the fourth quarter. Of course, the actual run was nothing out of the ordinary for Emmitt Smith. Like the thousands before it, Emmitt took the handoff, read the defense before taking his first step and hit the hole before it actually appeared.

Later in that same drive, Smith scored his 150th career touchdown on a signature one-yard hurdle over the pile. When he came to the Dallas sideline, he was greeted by one of his best friends, Michael Irvin, who was there with a giant hug. Most members of his family were there along with Daryl "Moose" Johnston, Emmitt's former leading blocker. Johnston, Fox's color analyst, gave him a hug and Emmitt couldn't contain himself any longer. The tears came without warning.

Emmitt's game day routine before entering Texas Stadium.

"That was simply one of those moments that I had no idea exactly how I'd react," Smith says. "I wanted to jump around and celebrate a lot more, but we had a game to win and I needed to compose myself long enough to get focused on the Seahawks."

From the opening kickoff, Emmitt ran like a man on a mission. Exploding on every play, Smith looked as if he'd accomplish the feat before halftime but Seattle stiffened their defense and gaining yardage proved tougher.

"I don't care what type of defense you have, no one wants to be the team a record is set against," Emmitt says. "Seattle played a very intense game because they didn't want to be the team in the record books. Even before the game, one of their defensive linemen was talking trash, telling me I wasn't going to set the record today. After I passed the record, he came up and congratulated me."

Emmitt's record-breaking run followed a Seattle scoring drive that gave the Seahawks a seven-point lead in the final quarter. The crowd erupted when Dallas took the field to start the record drive. By the time the record was within nine yards, you couldn't hear yourself think. Rookie quarterback Chad Hutchinson called "15 Lead". Emmitt did the rest, following fullback Robert Thomas. Before he knew it, Smith was in the Seahawks' secondary with the record in his wake. He then finished the drive with a one-yard dive for the tying score.

"It was very important to me to break the record at Texas Stadium because this is where it all began. It was important to do it in front of the home crowd, because making history of this magnitude is such a special thing."

"You have 64,000 people who shared this day with me and I hope I gave them something they can remember for the rest of their lives. It was a special moment for our fans and a great way to pay them back. It means a lot to do it in our house, where we are truly appreciated."

"My career is built around
a great group of players that have sacrificed
their bodies for the sake of the team."
— Emmitt Smith

Despite a tough loss to the underdog Seahawks, thousands of Dallas' faithful fans stuck around after the game to help Emmitt celebrate the milestone by watching a trophy ceremony, which ended in fireworks and the unveiling of a commemorative banner that will hang forever from the rafters of Texas Stadium.

"He's without peer and in this profession that means a heck of a lot," says Cowboys owner Jerry Jones. "Emmitt has been a great leader for our team for many years and is responsible for so many great moments, but I think this one tops them all. It's truly a magnificent accomplishment, one I don't think we'll see surpassed for a very long time."

For the last 13 seasons, Emmitt has made something extraordinarily complicated look simple. Opponents have never figured out how he does it. Teammates continue to marvel at his ability to do it.

"I have the ability to see and get there, the ability to really process information quickly," Smith says. "Some runners have tunnel vision. I am going right and that's it, nothing will change me. But they never see the other side away from the flow, which is the way I want to go even if the defense doesn't know it."

"It's uncanny, but Emmitt never ever takes a bad hit," says Daryl Johnston, who led the way for Emmitt through tough defenses for a majority of his career. "He sees the field so well and can anticipate what's going to happen a split second before it actually happens that he's able to avoid the big ones. It is truly amazing and only the very special players have that gift."

"He goes hard the entire game on every play," says teammate Darren Woodson, who along with Smith is the last of the Super Bowl-era Cowboys. "You might stop him for a while. You might stop him for an entire game. But he'll keep coming as if it's the first play of the game. He doesn't care. If a defense lets up for one second, he'll find a way to make you pay."

Emmitt Smith is the only running back in NFL history with 1,000 rushing yards or more for 11 consecutive seasons. He also carries the running back record for most rushing touchdowns. Of his 150 career touchdowns, 120 have come from within nine yards of the end zone. Forty-five have come from within a yard of the end zone.

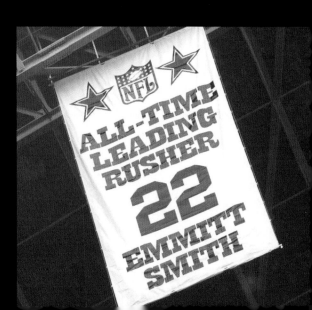

The Triplets — Troy Aikman, Emmitt Smith and Michael Irvin – will go down in the NFL annals as one of the most effective offensive combinations in history. The Cowboys also boasted one of the best offensive lines in football history.

"You can't single out one of those guys since all were part of my individual success and our success as a team," Smith says. "Larry Allen, John Gesek, Mark Stepnoski, Mark Tuinei, Erik Williams, Kevin Gogan and Ray Donaldson. Those are just some of the guys who deserve a share of this record."

"My career is built around a great group of players that have sacrificed their bodies for the sake of the team. Troy, Michael and I all benefited from that sacrifice."

You never know where you'll find your next franchise star. For the Cowboys, they found him in the first round of the 1990 NFL Draft. Jimmy Johnson liked the highlight tapes of Smith and wanted him wearing the silver and blue. Johnson explains: "All I saw of Emmitt was him making long runs against some of the best teams in the country in the SEC. That was enough to convince me that the young man was a football player. He wasn't the fastest or the biggest, but he could play the game when it counted and that's what we needed in Dallas."

While Johnson brought Emmitt to town, it was Cowboys offensive coordinator Norv Turner who turned him loose. Turner preaches ball-control offense and Smith enabled him to eat up the game clock and yardage, while setting up play-action passes for Aikman to his favorite targets, Irvin and tight end Jay Novacek.

"He gave me a workhorse, a guy we could give the ball to 30 times a game and he'd keep coming back for more," Turner says. "Emmitt wants to be the guy carrying the big load. He never backs away from the challenge even when the entire world knows we're going to hand him the ball. In fact, that's when it was fun. Everyone knew that our system was going to be run Emmitt until you could stop him. The thing was, no one could stop him."

How important is Emmitt Smith to the success of the Cowboys? Consider that he missed the first two games of the 1993 season and was replaced in the lineup by Derrick Lassic. Dallas lost its first two games. Upon Emmitt's return, the Cowboys marched to a division title, the NFC title and eventually another Super Bowl ring. Emmitt was the league and Super Bowl MVP that season.

With the team and individual success, in Emmitt's mind the `93 season really can be summed up in one game, a professional performance that would come to define the kind of player Emmitt James Smith III really is. Against the New York Giants at the Meadowlands, Emmitt rushed for 168 yards, caught 10 passes for 61 yards, and scored a touchdown, most of which came after he had separated his right shoulder in the second quarter. Dallas won the game in overtime, 16-13, after Emmitt literally carried the Cowboys down the field toward the winning field goal. It was the first opportunity to see Emmitt Smith's grit and determined attitude.

"That game probably defined who I was as a player at the time," Emmitt says. "The pain was worth it. We needed the win."

The similarity between Walter Payton and Emmitt Smith is obvious, as is the respect both shared for one another and the game. Both of these men share the type of determination rarely seen in any arena of professional sports. They earned their yardage in the middle of the field and never ducked out of bounds when staying in meant gaining an extra inch.

On the field, Payton played with unbridled passion. Off of it, he carried himself with dignity and grace, as does Smith. Emmitt recently received the Spirit of Sweetness Award, an honor named for Sweetness himself, Walter Payton.

"My only hope has always been that when I broke the record, he would be there," says Smith of Payton,

who passed away in 1999. "He was such a gracious man, a respectful man. He means so much to me. He was one of the guys that fueled me. He gave me a goal to shoot for. That is the saddest thing for me, knowing he wasn't there, knowing he has passed. When he did, it hurt me deeply to lose him because he meant so much to my family and me. Even though he never knew how much he meant to me, or to the sport, I will never forget how much we owe him."

It was no surprise that the tears flowed freely when Emmitt spoke of his hero on the floor of Texas Stadium after breaking Payton's record. The goal he had written down as a rookie so many years before had become reality. But even Emmitt's carefully planned, methodical assault on NFL history could not have prepared him for the sheer emotion of this moment. The stadium radiates with the love of his family and Walter's, and the admiration and respect of fans that know deep inside that this record will always belong to both men. Two men who held their team above all else, and in the relentless and pure pursuit of wins just happened to rack up over 16,700 yards each.

"The greatest compliment for me will be when the next guy comes along to break my record, and he feels the same way about me, as I feel about Walter," Emmitt J. Smith III.

Celebration party with Jerry Jones' family.

THE LEGENDS

"Every time I think about the list of
legendary running backs that I've passed
on this march, I get chills."
— Emmitt Smith

"Walter was an inspiration to me by the way he carried himself on and off the field. I admire him because of his work ethic, his love for the game, his love for his team and his athletic ability."
— Emmitt Smith

For the last several seasons, fans watched as Emmitt made his assault up the running back's version of Mount Rushmore. And each time he passed a Gale Sayers, a Franco Harris or a Tony Dorsett, the face-painting public nodded their approval and then quickly asked, "Who's next?"

Not that this is a news flash, but fans can be a fickle bunch. In the what-have-you-done-for-me-lately world of sports, records are no longer just made to be broken. Records — whether it's the single-season home run mark, the 100-meter dash or the all-time rushing record — are made to be smashed. And then smashed again and again until the public is satisfied that this performance is truly one for the ages. After all, Mark McGwire's once-in-a-lifetime season of 70

home runs lasted three whole seasons before Barry Bonds smacked 73. When will Alex Rodriguez or Jason Giambi smack 75 or 80? The fans are impatiently waiting.

So, yes, even before Emmitt established the new benchmark, fans immediately looked for the next running back with a chance to top him. Funny thing is, there isn't anyone remotely on his heels. Terrell Davis was off to a great start, got hurt and now is retired. Jerome Bettis is a workhorse, but he'll never make it. Marshall Faulk? His team throws the ball too much. Ricky Williams? Perhaps, if he stays healthy and plays 12 or 13 more seasons. That's an "if" the size of Texas. Maybe LaDainian Tomlinson, the second-year man from San Diego? He's off to a nice

Walter Payton - 16,726 yards

Jim Brown - 12,312 yards

"Jim Brown was a grinder;
no-nonsense running back;
strong willed and
strong minded."
— Emmitt Smith

start, although his size will make it difficult to sustain long-term success through the weekly beatings from defenses.

What Emmitt accomplished is amazing, not because it took a single burst of raw athleticism, but rather because it took thousands.

"I want to put that record so far out of sight that no one can touch it," Emmitt has said many times as he's approached Payton's mark.

But even Smith knows that eventually someone will come along with the talent and, more importantly, the strength of heart to write a new number in the record book. And when that day comes, that very special running back will look back at the legends he's passed with reverence, just as Emmitt does.

"Every time I think about the list of legendary running backs that I've passed on this march, I get chills," Emmitt says. "Playing running back at this level takes a special athlete and a special person. I have such respect for the men who have excelled at this position."

Men like Gale Sayers, whose silky smooth running style and explosive speed was prematurely taken from us because of injury.

Men like Franco Harris, who excelled on the biggest stage of all — the Super Bowl — for a team that made playing in January an annual routine.

"Playing running back at this level
takes a special athlete and a special person.
I have such respect for the men who have
excelled at this position."
— Emmitt Smith

Men like Marcus Allen, who would have rather dived over a pile for an extra inch than run out of bounds to save his skinny frame.

Men like Earl Campbell, who carried his team on his broad shoulders like no back in history, a workload that eventually cut short his career.

Men like Eric Dickerson, whose upright running style, goggles and a record-setting 2,000-yard season were trademarks of unmatched greatness.

Men like Barry Sanders, who shocked the NFL by walking away from a game he dominated and a record he most certainly would have demolished.

Men like Jim Brown, who shocked the NFL by walking away from a game he dominated because he wanted more from life than handoffs and touchdowns.

Men like Walter Payton, who played the game on the field and lived his life off the field as if there were no tomorrows. One day, much too soon, he was right.

Passing these men in the record books, especially Payton, gives Emmitt pause each and every time the question is raised.

"I've said it many times, but I'm honored to be mentioned with this group of legendary running backs," Emmitt says. "Watching Eric Dickerson carve up defenses with that upright running style. Seeing Earl Campbell run through linebackers to get a first down. Getting to see firsthand Barry Sanders make something big out of absolutely nothing with moves no running back has ever owned. Those are the types of performance and the types of men that deserve to be called legends."

Men like Emmitt Smith.

Gale Sayers - 4,956 yards

"Great speed, a good back but his career was
cut short because of injury."
— Emmitt Smith

Earl Campbell - 9,407 yards

"Powerful and bruising — he punished tacklers."
— Emmitt Smith

"Hard to tackle, great feet, balance, quickness,
leg strength and great start and re-start ability."
— Emmitt Smith

John Riggins - 11,352 yards

"Work horse, ultimate hog."
— Emmitt Smith

Thurman Thomas - 12,074 yards

"Created era of all purpose back, very versatile."
— Emmitt Smith

Franco Harris - 12,120 yards

"He was always at the right place at the right time."
— Emmitt Smith

Marcus Allen - 12,243 yards

"His toughness; how he made
the transition from fullback to running back.
He had great hands and a nose for the end zone."
— Emmitt Smith

Tony Dorsett - 12,739 yards

"Great vision, great speed
and a great all-around player."
— Emmitt Smith

Eric Dickerson - 13,259 yards

"A very graceful runner.
He made the game look effortless."
— Emmitt Smith

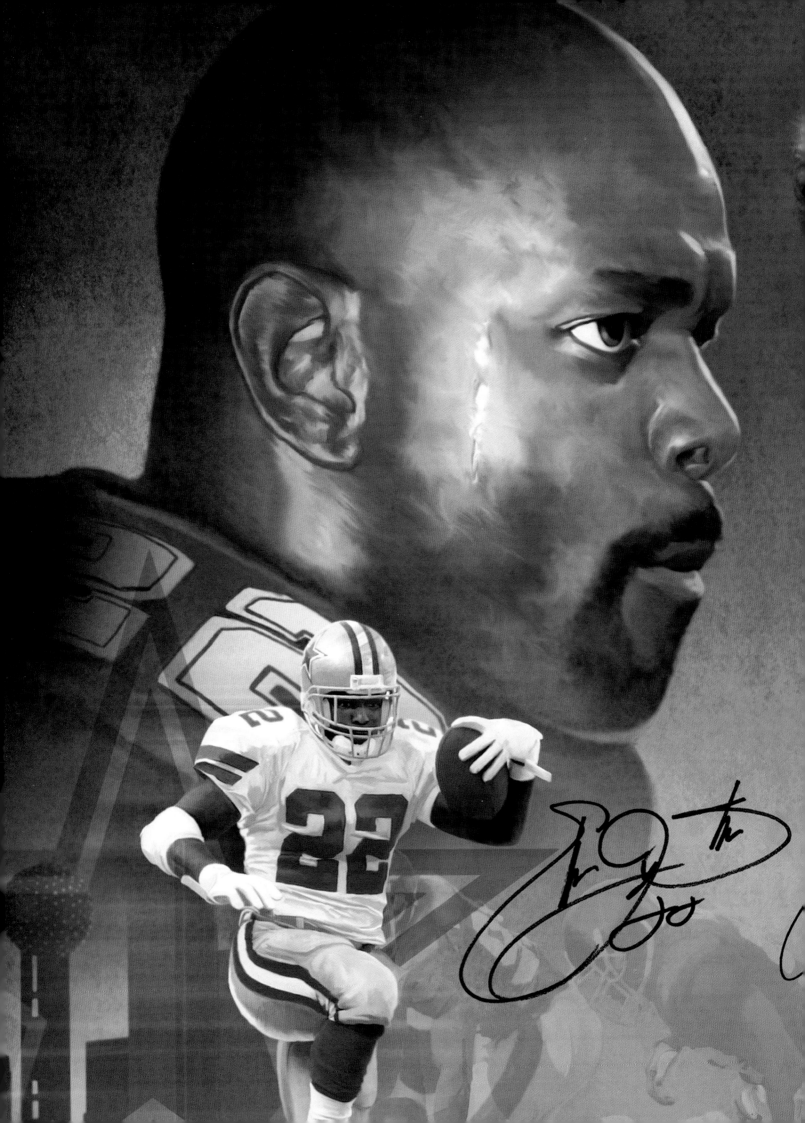

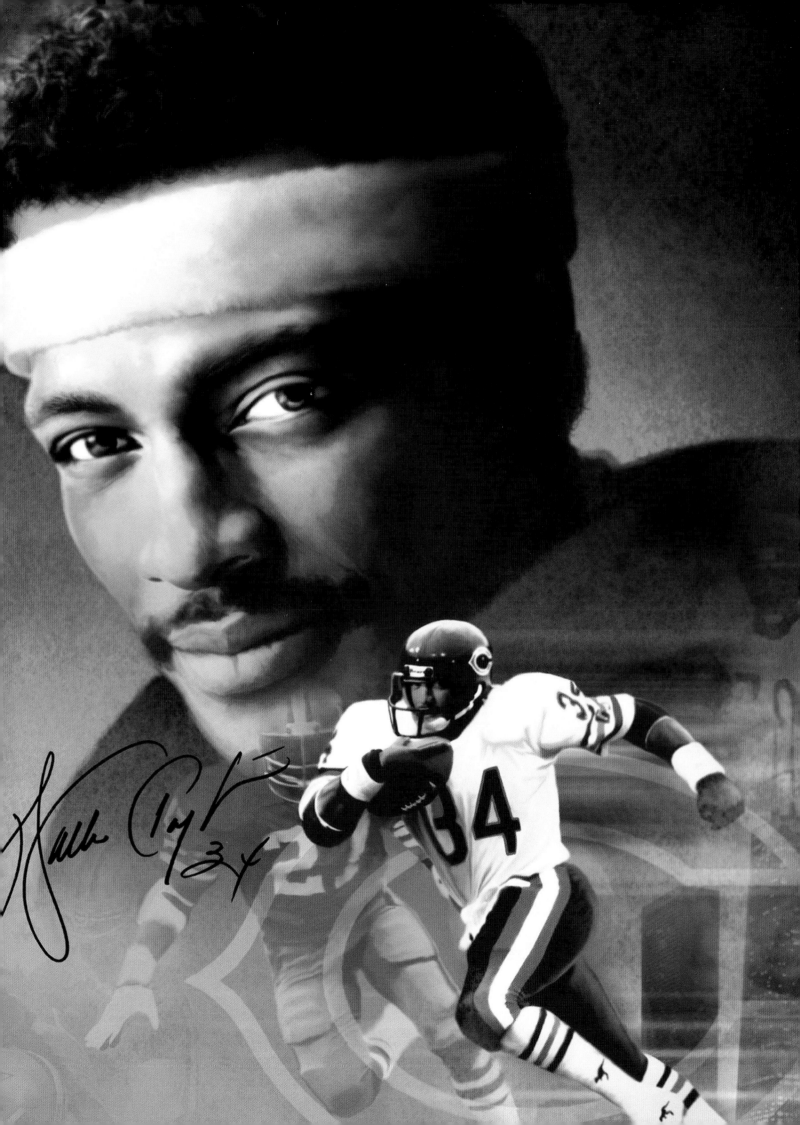

THE DEFINING MOMENTS

"I gave my first touchdown ball
to our equipment guy to keep
for me because my dad told me
you never know where
you will end up in history."

— Emmitt Smith

"My body hasn't stopped hurting since
I first pulled on a pair of shoulder pads.
Football is not for the weak of mind or heart.
You either put it on the line or you
take up another sport."
— Emmitt Smith

Head tucked low. Body taut. Ready to explode. The count. The snap. The play unfolds. Emmitt Smith uncurls from his customary spot in the eye of the backfield and takes the ball. Two quick steps toward the line and there's nowhere to go. His right guard has been blown back toward him by a pit bull of a defensive tackle. Emmitt jukes the behemoth and dashes outside to a sliver of daylight. He dives forward as he's hit by a 300-pound freight train and two of his sizable cohorts. By the time the referee pulls everyone off the pile of humanity at the 35-yard line, Emmitt's gained four yards. The announcer says "2nd and 6" and the Cowboys huddle for the next play.

And so it goes for Emmitt Smith. Yards, inches, centimeters. They all matter. They all count. It's just that some feel a whole lot better than others. In the scheme of things, it's just one carry in more than 10,000 in Smith's football career. He's spent a majority of his life looking at the world from the same vantage point — three steps directly behind the quarterback, crouched and ready to strike.

Out of the thousands of carries in Emmitt's football life, how many actually define him as a football player? 10? 100? 1,000? In truth, the answer is that every last one of them helped shape the legendary running back. But when push comes to shove — which is always the case in this relentless game of football — four games in particular define No. 22 like no other.

11.24.84

Escambia Gators vs. Tallahassee Rickards

Before he even donned No. 22, Emmitt Smith earned a reputation for ruggedness that remains today. Here's a guy who finds a way to fall forward no matter who — or how many — he runs into or what's on the line. After all, you don't rush for more than 16,000 yards by skipping out of bounds to save yourself. You can only reach such lofty milestones by driving hard every time you touch the ball by playing in pain more often than you care to recall.

"My body hasn't stopped hurting since I first pulled on a pair of shoulder pads," Emmitt says. "Football is not for the weak of mind or heart. You either put it on the line or you take up another sport."

As a sophomore at Escambia High, Smith flashed the type of guts it takes to be the very best. Playing on a severely sprained ankle, Emmitt rushed for 80 yards and scored a touchdown. The performance sparked the Gators to a triple-overtime victory against Tallahassee Rickards, 26-23, to advance to the second round of the state playoffs. It was a victory march that didn't end until Escambia had claimed its first-ever state title — the first of two consecutive in the Emmitt Smith era.

Emmitt had injured his ankle during the week leading up to the game against Rickards. The ankle was so tender that Escambia's coaches chose not to play him in the first half, much to Rickards' relief.

"But at halftime, Emmitt came up to us and told us to tape him up, he was going in," remembers Escambia's head coach Dwight Thomas. "Emmitt is one of the toughest people I've ever come across. Not playing was bringing him to tears. He just had to get in there and make a difference."

Escambia had been unable to move the ball throughout the first half, but after Emmitt checked in, the Gators began a critical drive that he capped with a 10-yard touchdown run to tie the game and force overtime.

Although it marked one of the four games in Smith's high school career that he didn't top the century mark, the performance ranks at the top of his personal highlight reel of games.

"Sometimes the yards come easy and those are the games that you tend to forget," Smith says. "But games like that, when the chips are stacked against you and you're giving it everything, those are why you play football. Believe me, the pain was worth it."

09.19.87

Florida vs. Alabama

Since the dawn of time — or at least from the moment Bear Bryant arrived in Tuscaloosa — Alabama football defined the Southeast. No matter what the records or the situation, a game against the Crimson Tide was much more than something you chalked up in the win/loss column. A game against Alabama was a way to send a message to everyone in the region and the country.

Emmitt Smith decided to step on this stage of stages and deliver a message that still reverberates around Legion Field. If there was ever a coming-out party, this was it.

Two days before the game, Florida head coach Galen Hall chose this freshman named Smith as his starter. He had played Smith in the opening two games against Miami and Tulsa, but this was going to be his big chance to either win the position for good or continue to scrap it out with the other talented tailbacks. Smith's answer: 224 rushing yards as the Gators won, 23-14, in front of a stunned Crimson Tide crowd.

Ironically, it was another running back, wearing the red of Alabama, who was supposed to write the headlines that day. Heisman Trophy candidate Bobby Humphrey came into the game as the heralded superback that was slotted for greatness. And although he turned in a solid performance (73 yards on 19 carries), he was a mere sidebar to Smith's epic story.

After dismantling Alabama, Emmitt continued his assault with six consecutive 100-yard games. His 1,341 rushing yards were a single-season Florida record and marked the third-best output ever from a freshman. Only Hershel Walker at Georgia and Tony Dorsett at Pittsburgh turned in better opening seasons. Smith finished ninth in that year's Heisman contest, which was the second-highest finish for a freshman in history.

He may not have claimed the Heisman, but he did solidify his spot as the No. 1 back. Shortly after the Alabama game, both of Florida's other talented tailbacks — Lloyd Hopkins and Octavius Gould — transferred.

01.31.93

Cowboys vs. Bills, Super Bowl XXVIII

> "I was lucky to be on such a great team.
> I'm just glad that I was able to do my part,
> because all the individual awards
> mean nothing without the ring."
> — Emmitt Smith

Marv Levy is a good man. Some would go as far as saying he's great. He's considered one of the best NFL head coaches ever and one of the most beloved players' coaches in history. But when two words are mentioned, Levy can't help but cringe a little.

Super Bowl.

As in a big fat doughnut hole in four tries for his Buffalo Bills.

Levy's teams were explosive on offense and talented on defense. They had strong special teams and good work ethics. They were well conditioned, well practiced and well prepared for each game. And each time they reached the big game, it all fell apart.

The first time it was wide right by about the length of a snow shovel.

The second time it was a missing helmet and an injured quarterback.

The third time it was a rabid opponent showing the world why successful college coaches with perfect hair can also dominate at the next level.

The fourth time it was Emmitt Smith, plain and simple.

Smith dealt Levy his fourth and final Super Bowl low blow in Atlanta in a game that will be remembered for a drive in which Emmitt carried the ball seven

times out of eight plays and the Cowboys scored a back-breaking touchdown.

It wouldn't have surprised anyone if the Cowboys walked into the Georgia Dome a tad overconfident against Buffalo. After all, it was just 12 months ago in Pasadena that most of these same Cowboys embarrassed the Bills, 52-17, in Super Bowl XXVII. Perhaps that's why Buffalo looked like they had caught Dallas sleepwalking through the first half and had the game tied at 13 into the third quarter. If not for a pair of James Washington turnovers — one of which Washington returned for a touchdown — the Cowboys would have been in miserable shape.

In the third quarter, Dallas called "Power

Right" seven times. And each time, Emmitt followed his massive wall of blockers and rumbled through the Bills. His 15-yard touchdown run put the Cowboys up by seven points, but in truth, the game was settled before he even broke the plane of the end zone.

"He put the team on his back on that drive and it really took the wind out of our sails," said Bills quarterback Jim Kelly. "We played a good game up until then, but we just couldn't recover from that long touchdown drive."

Dallas scored another touchdown to make the final 30-13, and Emmitt took home the Super Bowl MVP. It fit nicely on his mantel next to his league MVP trophy.

01.02.94

Cowboys vs. Giants

"In my mind this is still my
best game. I had to dig deep...
deeper than I thought I could go."
— Emmitt Smith

When the 1993 season began, some Dallas fans incorrectly labeled Emmitt Smith as selfish. After all, his contract dispute and holdout did cost him two games and the Cowboys two victories. And two losses meant plenty in football's best division.

So by the time Dallas visited the Meadowlands on the final week of the regular season to decide the fate of the NFC East, fans felt as if Emmitt owed them something. He paid them back with interest.

Smith accounted for 229 of the Cowboys' 339 yards and scored his team's only touchdown. His 168 rushing yards clinched his third straight NFL rushing title and his 61 yards on 10 receptions out-produced the combined efforts of Michael Irvin and Alvin Harper.

So, it was a pretty nice statistical day for Emmitt. What made it his defining professional moment was the fact that he played more than two quarters of the game with a separated right shoulder. Following a

46-yard run, safety Greg Jackson had thrown Emmitt to the concrete-like surface of Giants Stadium, injured his shoulder.

"There were times in the game when I could actually hear the bones cracking. I knew it wasn't good, but I had to continue to play," Emmitt remembers. "When the linemen asked me if I was OK, I lied and told them yes every time."

In overtime, Smith carried the ball nine times to set up a winning field goal by Eddie Murray. The victory clinched the divisional title and home field advantage through the playoffs for Dallas and clinched something far greater for its running back.

"I think before January 2, 1994, I was known mostly as a good back that played for the money and that's about it," said Emmitt, who spent the night after the game in a Dallas hospital hooked up to IVs. "Now, I'm known as a player who will lay it all on the line for his teammates."

THE EARLY YEARS

"Emmitt was part of our youth movement. In his
first game, I knew I had someone special."
— Dwight Thomas,
Escambia High School head coach

"It's a dream until you write it down,
then it's a goal."
— Dwight Thomas,
Escambia High School head coach

Like any coach who blows his whistle more often than a train conductor, Dwight Thomas had a million different methods to motivate his young charges. There were quotes from famous generals and legendary coaches. There were inspirational speeches after practice and before they stormed out of the tunnel. And there were note cards. Yes, note cards.

"It's a dream until you write it down," Thomas would say. "Then it's a goal."

When Thomas handed Emmitt Smith his first blank note card before his freshman season at Escambia High, the pair took a quick look at the Florida high school record book and knew exactly what Emmitt would write.

People who live in the town of Pensacola, Florida, set their clocks by two seasons — football season and off-season. For the Gators of Escambia High School, the intense pressure to win on the gridiron is especially tough since the kids who play on Friday nights wear the same mascot name on their jerseys as do the state's fabled college team just up the road in Gainesville.

In 1983, after suffering through more losing than any high school deserves, Escambia head coach Dwight Thomas finally felt he had discovered the answer to his football prayers. His name was Emmitt Smith.

Like all good prep coaches, Thomas made it a practice to keep close tabs on the various middle school players in his area. And upon meeting them, the kids would look like, well, kids. Then along came a different breed of kid.

"Most kids that age would be wearing jeans or clothes that were sloppy," Thomas said. "I remember Emmitt came up and introduced himself to me, and he was wearing nice pants and nice shoes — not tennis shoes — and he looked real neat."

Thomas quickly learned that Emmitt owned even more substance than style.

Emmitt shows off for the camera.

Erik (left) with older brother Emmitt.

Emmitt's high school teammates at Escambia helped
propel No. 24 to the top of the prep ranks.
(10 - Cedric Allen, 12 - John Brady, 44 - Mark Manela, 81 - Allen Moore,
30 - Robert Malden, 75 - Alvis Collins, 73 - Jerry Sewell, 66 - John Endacott,
54 - Mark Johnson, 71 - Mark White, 80 - Reggie Johnson)

In his first game as a freshman, Smith carried the ball 11 times for 115 yards and two touchdowns against Pensacola Catholic. With those types of numbers, Thomas quickly considered installing a new dress code for the entire squad.

"Emmitt was part of our youth movement," Thomas said. "We started 11 sophomores and two freshmen that season. In his first game, I knew I had someone special."

Escambia finished that season 7-3, its first winning slate in seven long years. But it was merely the start of something special. The Gators won the 3-A state championship in 1984 thanks in large part to an amazing season that saw Emmitt rush for 2,424 yards and score 26 touchdowns.

By the time Escambia posted a perfect 13-0 record and claimed a second state title the following year, Emmitt's name was known on college campuses from coast to coast. Although the good folks of Gainesville no doubt would have preferred anonymity for this Pensacola gem, Emmitt's junior season could not helped but get noticed. A state-record 2,918 yards gave Smith the state's all-time rushing crown before he took his first handoff as a senior. He added 33 touchdowns for good measure.

Emmitt's grandfather, aunt Ollie-May,
mother and sister, Marsha,
help celebrate another award.

"I would have cut down on the phone calls," said Emmitt's father, Emmitt Jr. "I would have definitely trimmed down on the number of times that phone rang."

The Smiths lived in a modest brick house on North G Street. His father, Emmitt Jr., drove a bus for the city transit service and his mother, Mary, worked in loan services at Southern Home Savings Bank. No line of work could have prepared them for the avalanche of publicity and college propaganda that followed their son's every move.

"Emmitt handled the chaos very well," said Sheila Montgomery, one of Smith's high school math teachers. "He was very calm and collected about his success."

A third state championship was not in the cards, however, as Escambia's archrivals, Pensacola High, beat the Gators, which prevented them from reaching the playoffs. Emmitt's individual glory continued as he won national Player of the Year honors with another special season (1,937 yards and 28 touchdowns).

After four seasons and 1,127 carries, Smith totaled an astounding 8,804 yards — the third highest total ever in the nation at that time — and 106 touchdowns. His 7.8 yards per carry average reads like a typo.

Scoey isn't the name you read about very often when you peruse the latest Emmitt Smith story in *ESPN — The Magazine* or *Sports Illustrated*. But to his family, Emmitt is and forever will be Scoey.

It surprises no one to learn that Emmitt grew up with strong discipline and great moral fiber. His parents impressed upon him early and often that the golden rule is more than just a cute catchphrase.

"Emmitt was the guy everyone wanted to be around. He's the one everyone wanted to be like," said Demetri Wynne, who attended middle school and

"I told my dad I was going to be a running back for the Dallas Cowboys when I was six years old. I am living proof that dreams do come true."
— Emmitt Smith

Emmitt with his mother and father on National Signing Day.

Emmitt's best friend in high school and freshman
college roommate, Johnny Nichols.

"My high school years were
the purist and most innocent years
of football. We played for the love
of the game and each other."
— Emmitt Smith

high school with Smith. "But he never acted like a star. He was a great person and nothing ever changed him."

Scoey, if you must know, is a family nickname derived from Mary Smith's favorite entertainer at the time, Scoey Mitchell. When you're the third in a line of Emmitt's, it tends to get confusing around the house when everyone sits down for dinner. Of course, no one outside the family calls Emmitt by any other name, except maybe Mr. Smith or MVP.

Ironically, the Emmitt Smith legacy began at Packer Stadium. That's right, Packer Stadium. This was no frozen tundra, though. It was the home field for the Belleview Youth Association League and Emmitt soon owned the turf against his fellow 7 and 8-year-olds. Today, the field is called Emmitt Smith Stadium and his No. 45 hangs from the scoreboard.

"From the first time he started playing, we knew he was something special," said Emmitt Jr., in one of the rare instances in which a father was *not* overrating his son's athletic prowess.

Galen Hall didn't know Scoey Mitchell from Scooby-Doo. But he did know plenty about Emmitt Smith, the most sought-after recruit in the nation who just happened to reside in his backyard. Hall, the University of Florida head coach, won the sweepstakes in large part because of the obvious — Emmitt's parents didn't have to travel far to see their son play.

"We were thrilled to get him because the process was extremely competitive," Hall said. "When you do the types of things Emmitt did in high school, every big school in the country is ready to throw their doors wide open. We just fell into it since we were next-door neighbors."

When Smith arrived in Gainesville, he was third on the depth chart behind two returning tailbacks. But when the first-string defense couldn't seem to do anything with Emmitt in practice, Hall knew he needed to get the freshman some playing time right away.

"I spent three of the best years of my life at the University of Florida. I made a bunch of lifelong friends and although it was time to go to the next level, I knew I was going to get my degree."
— Emmitt Smith

His first college action came against eventual national champion Miami. Emmitt touched the ball just five times for 16 yards. Skeptics said this wouldn't be the cakewalk that high school represented. But in his next game against Tulsa, Smith looked as if he was back at Escambia with 109 yards on 10 carries, including a 66-yard touchdown gallop.

Hall had seen enough to award Smith the starting nod against Alabama. Emmitt thanked him by rushing for 224 yards and two touchdowns on 39 carries as the Gators shocked the 11th-ranked Crimson Tide in Birmingham, Alabama.

Smith hit the 1,000-yard plateau after seven games, faster than any freshmen in NCAA history. He was holding national media conference calls every week and his name was prominently displayed on the Heisman ballot.

Basically, Emmitt's freshman orientation was perfect. Unfortunately, his college career never exceeded that flawless opening act. He injured his knee

as a sophomore and missed two games. He still managed 988 rushing yards for the season and piled on 159 more in the Gators' bowl game. As a junior, Emmitt established a school rushing record with 1,599 yards. Somehow he finished a distant seventh in the Heisman voting to Oklahoma's Billy Sims.

But more than losing out on the individual hardware, Smith's junior season was marred by rumors of wrongdoings with the Florida program. The Gators came under scrutiny of the NCAA and eventually four players were suspended for gambling on college football games. Emmitt calls the season the most frustrating of his football career. That's why the decision to turn pro wasn't a difficult one.

"I spent three of the best years of my life at the University of Florida," Smith often says. "I made a bunch of lifelong friends and although it was time to go to the next level, I knew I was going to get my degree."

Emmitt's best friend in college, Terence Barber.

THE CHASE

"I remember my first game like it was yesterday.

I can't believe how many great moments

I have to look back on in my career.

I am truly blessed."

— Emmitt Smith

Emmitt rushes for 937 yards to lead all rookies and scores 11 touchdowns, his first on Sept. 23 in RFK Stadium against the Redskins. He is voted NFL Offensive Rookie of the Year and plays in his first Pro Bowl. Emmitt's emergence brings balance to the offense and completes The Triplets — Smith, Troy Aikman and Michael Irvin.

937 yds, 15,789 yds to go

1990

ROOKIE OF THE YEAR

"I really wanted the Rookie of the Year.
I didn't win the Heisman, and I wanted
to show people that questioned whether
I could play at the next level that I was for real!"
— Emmitt Smith

No Cowboys back ever led the league in rushing until Emmitt accomplishes the feat this season with 1,563 yards. At 22 years old, Smith is the youngest player in history to surpass 1,500 yards in a single season. Emmitt's 75-yard touchdown dash against Washington on Sept. 9 is the longest run from scrimmage in the NFL this season. Against Atlanta in the Cowboys final regular season game, Smith goes for 160 yards to edge Thurman Thomas and Barry Sanders for the rushing title. Dallas qualifies for the playoffs for the first time since Jimmy Johnson and Jerry Jones introduced themselves to Texas, and Emmitt makes his second trip to Honolulu for the Pro Bowl.

2,500 yds, 14,226 yds to go

1991

NFL RUSHING TITLE No. 1

"There's so much talent at this level,
to win this title was a real honor."
— Emmitt Smith

In what becomes one of the Cowboys greatest-ever campaigns, Emmitt leads the league in rushing yards (1,713), rushing touchdowns (18) and total touchdowns (19). The season also marks the first time Mr. Smith put his name on the same page as a certain former Bears running back nicknamed Sweetness. Emmitt becomes the first player since Walter Payton to post consecutive 1,500-yard seasons. Of course, the true sweet part of this season comes in January when Dallas wins Super Bowl XXVII with a 52-17 humiliation of the Buffalo Bills. Smith is the first Dallas player to rush for more than 100 yards in a Super Bowl with 108 vs. the Bills.

4,213 yds, 12,153 yds to go

1992

N F L   R U S H I N G   T I T L E   No. 2

"Lots of guys have great years.

I wanted to be someone my team

could count on every single play."

— Emmitt Smith

Smith tops his marvelous 1992 season with a year for the ages. He wins league and Super Bowl MVP honors and claims his third consecutive rushing crown. On Halloween against the Eagles, Emmitt rushed for an amazing 237 yards to become the first player since, you know who, to hit such a lofty level. Payton's 275-yard performance against the Vikings in 1977 was a league record until recently. Smith crossed the 5,000-yard career-rushing milestone against the Dolphins on Thanksgiving Day. On the season's final day at the Meadowlands in New Jersey, Emmitt put in a performance that defined the team player that he is. Playing with a separated shoulder, he rushed for 168 yards and caught 10 passes to carry the Cowboys over the Giants. Then in Super Bowl XXVIII again vs. Buffalo, Emmitt hoisted the team on his back in the second half as Dallas scored 24 unanswered points and beat a tough Bills team, 30-13. No. 22 was off to Disney World.

1993

N F L   R U S H I N G   T I T L E   No. 3

"We work hard as a team so we
can be consistent. Winning three in a row
was special because of the standard
I wanted to keep for myself each year."
— Emmitt Smith

1993

SUPER BOWL XXVIII MVP

"All you want each season is a ring.
When I found out that I won the MVP,
it was truly the icing on a great year."
— Emmitt Smith

Although this season was good for Emmitt personally, it was a tough year for the team. Emmitt established an NFL high for rushing touchdowns with 22, which was his best personal season. But his team was dealt one of its toughest setbacks in franchise history when it lost in the NFC title game to the San Francisco 49ers. The defeat ended any chances at a three-peat and thrust onto center stage another successful college coach who Jones pegged to lead his franchise into the future. Playing under first-year coach Barry Switzer, Emmitt struggled with hamstring maladies throughout the season. Regardless, he made his fifth-straight Pro Bowl and scored 132 points.

Since he pulled on his first shoulder pads, Emmitt has been a touchdown-scoring machine. In this Super Bowl season, he set the new standard for the NFL. Smith's 25 rushing touchdowns broke John Riggins' previous mark of 24 set in 1983 and the Cowboys claimed their third world title in four years. Emmitt again led the league in rushing with 1,773 yards. But his greatest performances of the season came in the postseason as Smith scored three touchdowns and ran for 150 yards to beat back the Packers in the NFC title game. In Super Bowl XXX against the lovable underdogs, the Pittsburgh Steelers, Emmitt scored a second-half touchdown in Dallas' 27-17 victory.

8,956 yds, 7,770 yds to go

1995

NFL RUSHING TITLE No. 4

"This was a big year for me.
I really got to touch the ball a lot
and was glad that I could be
productive for the team."
— Emmitt Smith

Despite things spinning out of control for some of his Cowboys teammates, Emmitt maintained his focus and turned in another solid season. He finished fourth in the rushing race despite several nagging injuries and put together a fantastic performance against Minnesota in the Wild Card round of the playoffs (116 yards on 17 carries and two touchdowns). The scores gave Emmitt an NFL-record 18 career rushing touchdowns in the postseason and marked his eighth consecutive postseason game with a touchdown — another NFL first. Following the season, Smith underwent surgery to remove three bone fragments from his right ankle.

10,160 yds, 6,566 yds to go

1997

This was a critical season in Emmitt's personal march up the mountain toward Payton's all-time rushing record. He was coming off of a delicate ankle surgery and he was fighting something few running backs overcome — age. The lifespan for the typical NFL running back is 2.5 seasons. This was Emmitt's eighth. And despite the ankle surgery, a bum shoulder suffered against the Cardinals in December and even the flu bug against the Bengals, Smith's relentless pursuit continued strong. His seventh consecutive 1,000-yard season, Emmitt finished with 1,074 yards, pushed him past 11,000 for his career. Only 10 other men could say the same.

16,726

15,000

10,000

5,000

1,000

11,234 yds, 5,492 yds to go

With a healthier body, Emmitt was re-energized for the '98 campaign. He rushed for 1,332 yards, scored 13 touchdowns and was voted to his seventh Pro Bowl. His numbers were starting to become staggering. He was passing legends such as Tony Dorsett in the Cowboys' record books practically every week. He was passing NFL luminaries such as John Riggins, Marcus Allen and O.J. Simpson in the league's record books as well. On a 32-yard run in the second quarter on Nov. 8 against the Giants, Emmitt became the Cowboys' all-time leading rusher with 12,037 yards. In the season finale, Smith's two rushing touchdowns gave him 125 for his career, leap-frogging Allen for first on the all-time list.

12,566 yds, 4,160 yds to go

1999

Think about taking 3,000 handoffs in the NFL. That's 3,000 times 11 men trained to hurt you zeroed in on you for bodily harm. In '99, Smith became just the fourth player in league history to carry the ball 3,000 times. He also passed Tony Dorsett again, moving into fourth place on the all-time NFL rushing list. This season was truly special for Emmitt, despite his team's lackluster finish in the playoffs against the Vikings. He totaled 1,397 yards and ranked second in the NFC in rushing. Just to top it off, Emmitt emerged as the NFL's all-time leading postseason ground gainer (1,586 yards) and its leader in postseason rushing touchdowns (19).

In 2000, Emmitt crossed the century mark against the Eagles for the 12th time in his career. It's the most 100-yard games for any player against a single opponent in league history. His 1,203 rushing yards for the season earned him yet another trip to Honolulu, his ninth such honor. Only Mr. Cowboy, Bob Lilly (11) and Mel Renfro (10) were named to more Pro Bowl squads.

With a rookie quarterback, a battered and inexperienced offensive line, no Moose and hobbled receivers, Emmitt Smith rushed for another 1,000-yard season. Enough said. Except, there's plenty more to be said about this phenomenal running back. Emmitt is the first NFL runner ever to compile 11 1,000-yard rushing seasons and he did it in 11-consecutive seasons. He passed Barry Sanders' record of 10 consecutive 1,000-yard seasons in Barry's backyard of Pontiac, Mich. His combined net yardage surpassed the 18,000-yard mark, which is basically the length of three golf courses. Against San Diego on September 23, Emmitt moved past Barry Sanders to the No. 2 spot on the all-time rushers list with a 14-yard run in the second quarter. Now, only Walter Payton remained.

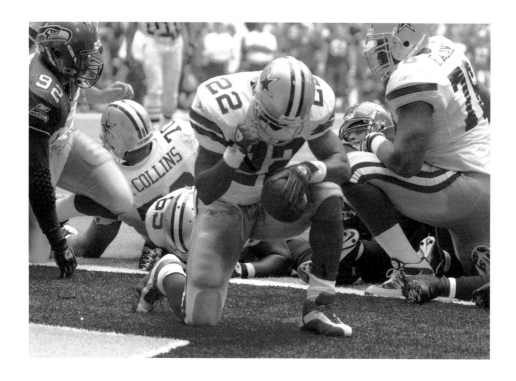

For many, this season will be remembered for one 11-yard burst through the left side of the line at Texas Stadium against the Seattle Seahawks in a play called "15 Lead". The result was a first down midway through the fourth quarter, and a record that may never be surpassed. Emmitt became the NFL's all-time leading rusher, passing Walter Payton's record on Sunday, October 27, 2002. The celebration will last a lifetime.

With former teammates such as Michael Irvin and Daryl Johnston looking on, Emmitt gave a speech about his record-breaking run. "Today was a special day. But I just can't pat myself on the back, because so many people were instrumental to this journey. I don't know how long it's going to last, because you're dealing with some unique circumstances. I don't know if you're going to find someone who will do it with one team like Walter did it and like I did it."

What's next for the greatest running back ever to lace up a pair of cleats? His mind and body tell him more carries, more yards and with some help from his teammates, more Cowboys' championships.

109

16,727 yds, and still going

THE MAN

"My most memorable evening

in Dallas was the visit of a young

lady who would eventually

become my wife."

— Emmitt Smith

"There's nothing more important than my family. It's always been that way and always will be."
— Emmitt Smith

Emmitt enters his living room for an exclusive photo shoot. Less than 72 hours before he runs for the biggest and most prestigious rushing record in NFL history, his manner is contemplative. His mood shifts from intense to jovial when his wife, Pat, and children enter the room.

"I'm just so blessed to have him," his wife Pat boasts. "As a husband, he's just totally committed to making me happy and being the best provider — a friend and confidant and a supporter. As a father, he's incredible."

"His wife and his children are the most important part of his life and everything he does is focused on making their lives better for the future," says his mother, Mary. "When you become a husband and especially a father, everything changes. Your perspective changes. Emmitt always wanted to know what was next. Now he knows."

Emmitt's wife and kids are the focus of this night. Pat, Jasmin (six), Rheagen (four) and Emmitt James Smith IV (five months) — or E.J. — surround Emmitt as they watch Playhouse Disney. His two young girls sprint around the house with nonstop energy. This is Emmitt relaxed.

"This is my life now," Emmitt says as Pat and the girls attack him with the feared Tickle Monster.

And life is good.

September 11th is a date that evokes powerful emotions for Americans. For Connie Payton, it has added significance. Connie happened to be staying in a Dallas hotel when the terrorists' attacks started. The phone rang not too long afterward. It was Emmitt Smith, inviting her to stay at his home.

The night before Emmitt received the Walter Payton Spirit of Sweetness Award, the Smiths and Paytons sat down for dinner. Emmitt sat across the

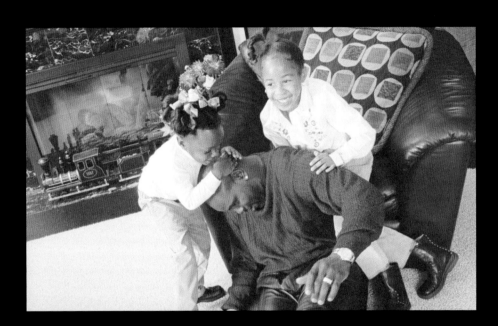

table from Jarrett, but before dinner he switched seats to sit next to the young man.

"He asked me if it was OK [to] call me from time to time just to check in. I said absolutely," Jarrett tells. "I couldn't believe it. Emmitt Smith wanted to call me?" The phone calls remain frequent between Dallas and The University of Miami where Jarrett is a running back for the Hurricanes.

"I told him I wanted to be a friend. I wasn't trying to replace his father. I'm just a good friend," Emmitt says. "There are some things a young man just doesn't want to discuss with his mom. He can open up to me about those things and I can try to give him advice. I never scold him. I just try to push him into the right direction."

Jarrett cherishes the relationship and never hesitates to reach out to Emmitt.

"I always had my dad to talk to about certain subjects and now I have Emmitt," Jarrett says. "Emmitt knows what I'm going through as a young man and helps me a lot. It's cool when Emmitt picks up the phone. He's actually excited to talk to me. That's pretty incredible."

"If it was someone else who broke my dad's rushing record, I might be upset, but not with Emmitt. It's OK that it's him."

When Marge Irwin first met Emmitt Smith, he had already won two Super Bowls, claimed a Super Bowl MVP and was one of the most well known players in the NFL.

All she remembers is that Emmitt reminded her a lot of her son.

"If I hadn't known what he looked like, I really don't think I would have thought he was even a professional football player," Marge recalls. "All I could think was here's a guy who acts just like my son, Kevin. He's very reserved and extremely polite. He was a good young guy who had his priorities in order."

Then Marge did something that few of us would ever think about. She volunteered to help someone move.

"Yeah, I know, my husband is still laughing about that one," Marge says. "Emmitt was building a home in Far North Dallas and he was about to start moving out of his apartment. I volunteered to help him get his stuff from one place to the other. I had no idea what I had committed to. I haven't volunteered for something like that again."

Marge left quite an impression, such that Emmitt hired her as his personal assistant. He even asked her to work out of his new house so that she could get a first-hand look at his daily life.

It was 1995 when Marge met Emmitt through her husband, Horace, who worked at the time for AMG, Emmitt's marketing agency. She moved out of the house when Emmitt married two years ago, but no one other than his wife and mother know more about Emmitt Smith than Marge.

"You might think this man would treat people differently because of who he is and what he's

"Watching my kids grow up is better than winning any games. I promise you that."
— Emmitt Smith

accomplished as a football player," Marge says, "that couldn't be further from the truth. Emmitt is just like a regular guy who really cares about people and this comes through with everyone he meets."

Emmitt's success on the field stems from hard work at practice coupled with gritty determination on game day. This has resulted in more than 16,743 yards.

"Emmitt always has been a well-disciplined and focused young man," says his mom. "We made sure he understood from a very young age that you must be responsible for your actions. We made sure he knew right from wrong and what would happen if he didn't stay on the right path. He's done nothing but make us proud."

Emmitt's pastor, Bishop Thomas D. Jakes, Jr., helps to guide this young man on that path.

Emmitt's favorite Bible verse is Proverbs 3:5-6, "Trust in the Lord with all your heart, and lean not on your own understanding; in all your ways acknowledge Him, and He shall direct your paths." Recently Emmitt acknowledged that God has really been directing his path.

"It has been a joy to serve as Emmitt's pastor and also to be his friend," Jakes says. "I have noticed

tremendous growth in him both as a Christian and as a person. He is a charitable man whose generosity and true nature has been exhibited in his many endeavors. I have seen him involved in outreach programs like feeding hungry children and sponsoring projects that made a difference in our community."

"Several years ago, I had the privilege of baptizing him. I am proud as his pastor to see that he has continued to practice his faith," Jakes continues. "He is a regular attendee of our services at The Potter's House in Dallas when he's not traveling. When he does travel, he often calls to check on myself, the service he missed and to let me know how he is progressing in his walk with God."

Everyone close to Emmitt shares a similar sense of pride. From his high school coaches to his professional teammates, his football ties remain strong and unbreakable. "Emmitt is one of those special kinds of people, the ones who make you a better person for knowing them," says Dave Campo, head football coach with the Dallas Cowboys. "They just don't make many men like Emmitt Smith."

"The best play their best when it matters most. Emmitt does that for sure," Campo says. "But Emmitt

does even more. He makes everyone around him better not by being a rah-rah guy. He's a man of few words. His actions speak for him and the other players understand that language loud and clear."

Of course, Emmitt doesn't limit his drive and intensity to just the playing field. He has long sought to be a successful businessman, even before he was an NFL star. Now he is reaching that goal as his playing career winds to a glorious close. Emmitt has joined forces with WeTrak Founder Tommy Davis to combat wide spread fraud in the memorabilia industry. WeTrak is one of the world's finest autograph and memorabilia security services.

Emmitt has been involved with The Open Doors Foundation, which helps underprivileged children realize their dreams. One click to emmittzone.com or an hour speaking to Emmitt reveals his dedication to the future through helping American children grow into the successful people that they strive to be.

"He sincerely cares about everyone, but especially kids that have had a rough upbringing," Marge says.

"On the football field, no one can find a soft spot on Emmitt. He's as tough as nails, no matter how big the other guy happens to be, but when he starts talking about kids, he's a big softie."

"There's nothing more important to me than my family. It's always been that way and it always will be so," Emmitt says. "My mother, father and grandmother instilled a special appreciation for family. My brothers and sisters are all tight. There's so much love that it's incredible."

"Now, as a husband and father, it's my turn to carry on what my family taught me," he says. "Watching my kids grow up is better than winning any game. I promise you that."

Emmitt Smith and Walter Payton are great athletes and special football players, but even better men.

"The NFL has been extremely fortunate to have had Walter and now Emmitt as two tremendous ambassadors for the league," Troy Aikman says.

We could not have said it better.

Preparing Emmitt's daily smoothie with
protein, fruit, mineral oil, and organic milk.

Emmitt gives emotional acceptance speech when receiving the Spirit of Sweetness award from the Payton family

Emmitt participating in Feed the Children and
The Open Doors Foundation event.

Emmitt's newest business venture - WeTrak.
The record breaking uniform was authenticated by
WeTrak a leading provider of Autographed and
memorabilia security services.

Thighs 27", Arms 17 3/4", Neck 17",
Helmet Large, VSR 4,Waist 34", Chest 48"

What's next for Emmitt? More of the same.

Statistics

Escambia High School

YEAR	ATT	YDS	AVG	TD
1983	256	1,525	5.9	19
1984	293	2,424	8.2	26
1985	353	2,918	8.2	33
1986	225	1,937	8.6	28

University of Florida

YEAR	ATT	YDS	AVG	TD
1987	229	1,341	5.9	13
1988	187	988	5.3	9
1989	284	1,599	5.6	14

Dallas Cowboys

YEAR	ATT	YDS	AVG	LONG	TD
1990	241	937	3.9	48t	11
1991	365	1,563	4.3	75t	12
1992	373	1,713	4.6	68t	18
1993	283	1,486	5.3	62t	9
1994	368	1,484	4.0	46	21
1995	377	1,773	4.7	60t	25
1996	327	1,204	3.7	42	12
1997	261	1,074	4.1	44	4
1998	319	1,332	4.2	32	13
1999	329	1,397	4.2	63t	11
2000	294	1,203	4.1	52	9
2001	261	1,021	3.9	44	3

Calverts celebrating the record breaking moment.

High school coach, Dwight Thomas, told Emmitt when you have a dream it is not a goal until you write it down. When Emmitt realized his goal of becoming the NFL's all-time rushing leader, The Calvert Group was able to reach a goal of its own. The Calvert Group established itself as a full-service publishing house thus expanding our services. Thank you Emmitt for helping others achieve their own goals!

The Calvert Group would like to acknowledge the following for their assistance and support:

Emmitt Smith family • Walter Payton family • Jeff Bernstein (JB) • Pro Access, Inc. staff • Werner Scott
Mary McKay• AMG staff • Marge Irwin • Lori Jones • Jerry Jones' family • Dallas Cowboys' staff • 4G² staff
Ron St. Angelo • Victor Grogan • Dan Sellers • Lorie Leigh Lawrence • Reagan White • Therese Bellar
9World staff • Bob Murray • Don Hess • Andrea Wildenthal • Callie LaFontaine • Monica Long
Encite Entertainment staff • Brad Berkley • Kim Branthoover • Mike Barker • Linda Egger • Betsy Holotik
Fred Vehon • Playbook Sports & Entertainment staff • Lara Beth Sampe • Carrie Gallow • Mark Harwell
Ryan Duckworth • Doug Anderson • Lori Peeraer • R.R. Donnelly Staff • Ben and Celeste Anderson
Quentin Smith • Heather and Troy Gingrich • Craig Ferris • Mike Montana • Raychel Calvert

The Calvert Group
thecalvertgroup.com
Chief Executive Officer: Randall Calvert
President/Creative Director: Carrie Calvert
Vice President: Craig Ferris
Senior Editor: Reagan White
Copy Editors: Heather and Troy Gingrich, Therese Bellar, Mike Biggs
Production Artist: Quentin Smith
PrePress: 4G²
Sales & Distribution: Encite Entertainment

Photo Credits
Ron St. Angelo: Cover, 1, 2, 3, 8, 9, 11, 12, 13, 15, 16, 19, 31, 35, 36, 43, 47, 67, 69,
71, 73, 75, 76, 79, 80, 81, 83, 84, 88, 89, 90, 91, 93, 94, 95, 96, 97, 98, 99,
100, 101, 102, 103, 104, 105, 106, 107, 108, 109, 122, 123, 124, 125, 126, 127
Lorie Leigh Lawrence: Family Photo Session, 4, 114, 117, 119, 128
4G²: 6, 7, 32, 33
Bryan Robley: 86, 87
Tom DiPace: 28, 29, 30, 41, 59, 62, 63, 64, 65
Emmitt Family: 5, 21, 49, 51, 52, 53, 54, 55, 56, 61, 111, 113, 120, 121
Gary McCracken, Pensacola News Journal: 38, 55, 58
Scott Cunningham: 68
Bob Rosato: 72
James D. Smith: 77
Paul Spinelli: 45
Corbis: 23, 24, 27, 29, 30, 31
Dallas Morning News: 15, 46

Stay informed, visit emmittzone.com